U.S. Fish & Wildlife Service

Predicting Wetland Functions at the Landscape Level for Coastal Georgia Using NWIPLUS Data

Cover: Salt marsh on Little St. Simons Island (R. Tiner photograph).

Predicting Wetland Functions at the Landscape Level
for Coastal Georgia Using NWIPlus Data

Ralph W. Tiner
Regional Wetland Coordinator
U.S. Fish & Wildlife Service
Northeast Region
300 Westgate Center Drive
Hadley, MA 01035

Prepared In Cooperation With the
Georgia Department of Natural Resources
Coastal Resources Division, Brunswick, GA and
Atkins North America, Raleigh, NC

August 2011

This publication should be cited as:

Tiner, R.W. 2011. Predicting Wetland Functions at the Landscape Level for Coastal Georgia Using NWIPlus Data. U.S. Fish and Wildlife Service, National Wetlands Inventory Program, Region 5, Hadley, MA. In cooperation with the Georgia Department of Natural Resources, Coastal Resources Division, Brunswick, GA and Atkins North America, Raleigh, NC. 29 pp.

Table of Contents

This page is intentionally blank.

Introduction

The Georgia Department of Natural Resources (GA DNR) has recently updated National Wetlands Inventory (NWI) data for the state's six coastal counties. The U.S. Fish and Wildlife Service (Service) has recognized the potential application of NWI data for watershed assessments, but realized that other attributes would have to be added to the data to facilitate functional analysis. In the early 1990s, Dr. Mark Brinson conceived a hydrogeomorphic approach to wetland functional assessment that uses comparison of field-verified properties of existing wetlands to those from a set of reference wetlands as a means of assessing a wetland's proximity to or departure from reference condition (Brinson 1993a). This approach provided the impetus for the Service to develop other attributes to expand the NWI database and make it more useful as a tool for landscape-level functional assessment of wetlands.

In the mid-1990s, the NWI developed a set of abiotic descriptors to describe a wetland's landscape position, landform, water flow path, and waterbody type (LLWW descriptors; Tiner 1995, 1996a, b). Use of the initial set of keys for pilot watershed projects led to a refinement and expansion of the keys in subsequent years (Tiner 1997a, b, 2000, 2002, 2003a). The expanded NWI database is called NWIPlus because it significantly increases the amount of information collected for mapped wetlands (Tiner 2010). These data allow for improved characterization of wetlands across the landscape and make it possible to predict wetland functions at the landscape, watershed, or regional scale. Numerous projects have created NWIPlus data and used the data to better describe wetlands in watersheds or other specific geographic areas and produce preliminary assessments of wetland functions (Table 1). In conducting these studies in the Northeast, the Service worked with local and regional wetland experts to develop relationships between wetland characteristics recorded in the database and wetland functions. The results reflect our best approximation of what types of wetlands are likely to perform certain functions at significant levels based on the characteristics in the NWIPlus database. Besides the Service's applications of these techniques, several states have been building NWIPlus or similar databases or have plans to conduct at least a pilot study including Kansas, Michigan, Minnesota, Montana, New Mexico, and Wisconsin (Tiner 2010). The State of Delaware has worked with the Service to update NWI data and create a statewide NWIPlus database, and will use the information to produce a series of reports on wetland status, recent and historic trends, wetland functions, and potential wetland restoration sites.

Table 1. Areas where the Service created a NWIPlus database and where functions have been analyzed or are planned for analysis. (* - functional assessment planned for 2011.)

State	Project Area	Approximate Area (square miles)
Alaska	Anchorage C7 quadrangle*	232
California	Ventura River watershed	232
Connecticut	entire state (planned)*	4,900
Delaware	entire state*	1,900
	Nanticoke watershed	490
Maine	Casco Bay	1,216
Maryland	Coastal Bays watershed	296
	Nanticoke watershed	323
Massachusetts	Boston Harbor and vicinity	232
	Cape Cod and the Islands	665
Minnesota	Fond du Lac reservation*	158
Mississippi	Coastal zone*	1,450
New Jersey	entire state*	7,500
	Hackensack River watershed	197
New York	Greater Buffalo area*	1,200
	Catherine Creek watershed	100
	Catskill watershed	571
	Croton watershed	391
	Cumberland Bay watershed	55
	Delaware River watershed	1,013
	Hackensack River watershed	197
	Hudson River-Snook Kill watershed	254
	Peconic River watershed	92
	Post Creek-Sing Sing Creek watershed	59
	Salmon River-So. Sandy Creek watershed	117
	Sodus Creek watershed	54
	Sodus Bay-Wolcott Creek watershed	65
	Sucker Brook-Grass River watershed	124
	Upper Tioughnioga River watershed	270
	Upper Wappinger Creek watershed	136
	Long Island*	1,400
Pennsylvania	Delaware River and Lake Erie coastal zones	113
Rhode Island	entire state*	1,100
South Carolina	Horry and Jasper Counties*	3,100
Texas	Corpus Christi area*	1,900
Vermont	Southern part of state*	580
Wyoming	Shirley Basin*	290

The State of Georgia recently added LLWW descriptors to their updated wetland inventory data to create an NWIPlus database for six coastal counties. The NWIPlus data will be used to better characterize wetlands in this region and to be able to predict wetland functions at the landscape level. In order to do the latter, the relationships (formerly called correlations) developed for use in the northeastern United States were introduced to and reviewed by a group of Georgia scientists from federal, state, and local agencies, non-profit organizations, and academic institutions at an August 31, 2010 workshop on Little St. Simons Island. The peer group provided comments that were used to re-evaluate the relationships and tailor them to coastal Georgia. In cases where there were differences in opinions, the points were considered and decisions were made by consensus between the Coastal Resources Division of the Georgia Department of Natural Resources, Atkins North America (formerly PBS&J Inc., Raleigh, NC), and Ralph Tiner (U.S. Fish and Wildlife Service, Region 5, Hadley, MA).

The purpose of this report is to explain how the NWIPlus data could be and was used for predicting wetland functions at the landscape-level for coastal Georgia and the rationale for assigning certain biotic and/or abiotic characteristics to eleven wetland functions: 1) surface water detention, 2) coastal storm surge detention, 3) streamflow maintenance, 4) nutrient transformation, 5) carbon sequestration, 6) sediment and other particulate retention, 7) bank and shoreline stabilization, 8) provision of fish and aquatic invertebrate habitat, 9) provision of waterfowl and waterbird habitat, 10) provision of other wildlife habitat, and 11) provision of habitat for unique, uncommon or highly diverse wetland plant communities.

Creating the NWIPlus Database

A set of abiotic attributes have been developed to increase the information contained in the NWI database and to create a NWIPlus database. Four groups of attributes describe:

- landscape position (relationship of a wetland to a waterbody if present: marine—ocean, estuarine—tidal brackish, lotic—river/stream, lentic—lake/reservoir, and terrene—not significantly affected by such waters, or no waterbody present, or the source of a stream);
- landform (physical shape of the wetland—basin, flat, floodplain, fringe, island, and slope);
- water flow path (inflow, outflow, throughflow, isolated, bidirectional-nontidal, and bidirectional-tidal); and
- waterbody type (different types of estuaries, rivers, lakes, and ponds).

Collectively, they are known as LLWW descriptors, which represent the first letter of each descriptor (landscape position, landform, water flow path, and waterbody type). Dichotomous keys have been developed to interpret these attributes (Tiner 2003b; they will be amended in 2011 to reflect results of recent applications). Other modifiers are also included in these keys to further describe wetland characteristics. LLWW descriptors are added to the NWI database by interpreting topography from digital raster graphics (DRGs) or digital elevation model data (DEMs), stream courses from the National Hydrography Dataset (NHD) and/or aerial imagery, and waterbody types from aerial imagery (Figure 1). The interpretations are done by employing some automated GIS-routines coupled with manual review and interpretation by wetland specialists. This effort now increases the NWI workload by less than 10 percent.

The NWIPlus database adds value and increases the functionality of the original NWI database. Besides providing more features that can be used to predict wetland functions from the NWI database, NWIPlus makes it possible to better characterize the nation's wetlands. For example, all the palustrine wetlands, which account for 95 percent of the wetlands in the conterminous United States, can now be linked to rivers, streams, lakes, and ponds where appropriate, so that the acreage of floodplain wetlands, lakeside wetlands, and geographically isolated wetlands can be reported. The Wetlands Subcommittee of the Federal Geographic Data Committee (FGDC) recognized the value added by the LLWW descriptors and recommended that they be included in wetland mapping to increase the functionality of wetland inventory databases (FGDC Wetlands Subcommittee 2009).

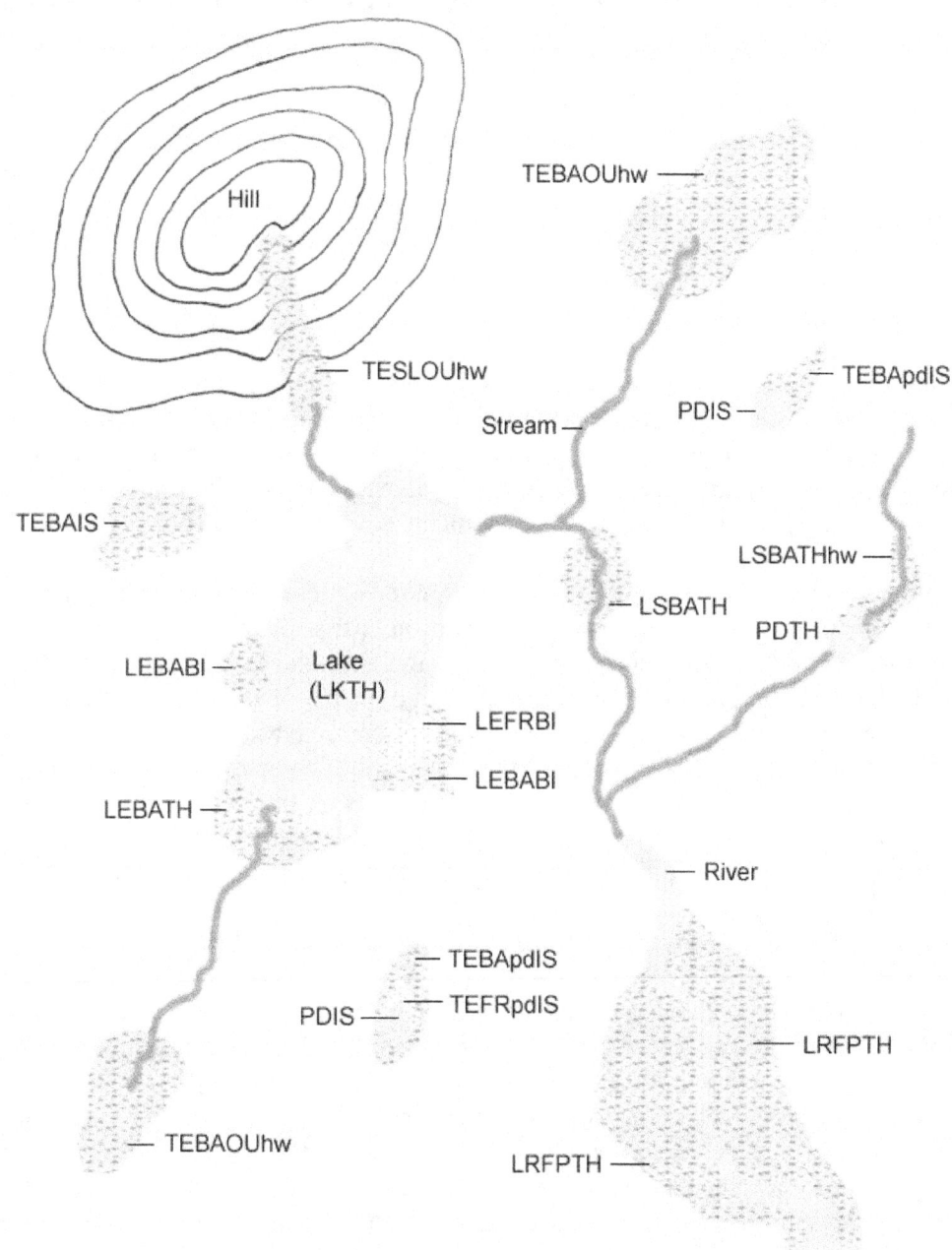

Figure 1. Examples of application of LLWW descriptors to nontidal wetlands. Coding: Landscape position = LE – Lentic, TE – Terrene, LR – Lotic River, LS – Lotic Stream; Landform = BA – Basin, FP – Floodplain, FR – Fringe, SL – Slope; Water Flow Path = BI – Bidirectional-nontidal, IS – Isolated, OU – Outflow, TH – Throughflow; Other descriptors: PD – Pond, LK – Lake, hw – headwater, and pd – pond-bordering wetland. <u>Note</u>: If desired, ponds and lakes can be further classified with landscape position resulting in codes of TEPDIS for the isolated ponds and LSLKTH for the lake shown in this figure.

Limitations of the Preliminary Wetland Functional Assessment

Source data are a primary limiting factor for landscape-level functional assessment. NWI digital data and existing stream data (e.g., National Hydrography Dataset) are used as the foundation for these assessments. All wetland and stream mapping has limitations due to scale, photo quality, date of the survey, and the difficulty of photointerpreting certain wetland types (especially evergreen forested wetlands and drier-end wetlands; see Tiner 1997c, 1999 for details) and narrow or intermittent streams especially those flowing through dense evergreen forests and beneath built-up lands.

Recognizing source data limitations, it is equally important to understand that this type of functional assessment is a preliminary one based on wetland characteristics interpreted through remote sensing and using the best professional judgment of various specialists to develop relationships between wetland characteristics in the database and wetland functions. It is designed for landscape- or watershed-level assessments covering large geographic areas.

Wetlands are rated based on their biotic or abiotic characteristics as having high or moderate potential for supporting a wetland function. Wetlands not assigned a rating are assumed to have little or no potential for providing such function at a significant level. The ratings are based on a review of the literature and best professional judgment by numerous scientists studying wetlands from public agencies, private non-government organizations, and academia. Also, no attempt is made to produce a more qualitative ranking for each function (comparing to a "reference" type representing a wetland of the type in the "best" condition, or on size or the degree to which it actually performs a function given opportunity and adjacent land uses) or for each wetland based on multiple functions as this would require more input from others and more data, well beyond the scope of this type of broad-scale evaluation. For a technical review of wetland functions, see Mitsch and Gosselink (2007) and for a broad overview, see Tiner (2005a).

Functional assessment of wetlands can involve many parameters. Typically such assessments have been done in the field on a case-by-case basis, considering observed features relative to those required to perform certain functions or by actual measurement of performance. The preliminary assessments based on remotely sensed information do not seek to replace the need for field evaluations since they represent the ultimate assessment of the functions for individual wetlands. Yet, for a watershed analysis, basin-wide field-derived assessments are not practical, cost-effective, or even possible given access considerations. For watershed planning purposes, a more generalized assessment (level 1 assessment) is worthwhile for targeting wetlands that may provide certain functions, especially for those functions dependent on landscape position, landform, hydrologic processes, and vegetative life form (Brooks et al. 2004). Subsequently, these results can be field-verified when it comes to actually evaluating particular wetlands for acquisition purposes (e.g., for conserving biodiversity or for preserving flood storage capacity) or for project impact assessment. Current aerial photography may also be examined to aid in further evaluations (e.g., condition of wetland/stream buffers or adjacent land use) that can supplement the preliminary assessment.

The landscape-level functional assessment approach -"Watershed-based Preliminary Assessment of Wetland Functions" (W-PAWF) - applies general knowledge about wetlands and their functions to develop a watershed overview that highlights possible wetlands of significance in terms of performance of various functions. To accomplish this objective, the relationships between wetlands and various functions are simplified into a set of practical criteria or observable characteristics. Such assessments may be further expanded to consider the condition of the associated waterbody and the neighboring upland or to evaluate the opportunity a wetland has to perform a particular function or service to society, for example.

W-PAWF does not account for the opportunity that a wetland has to provide a function resulting from a certain land-use practice upstream or the presence of certain structures or land-uses downstream. For example, two wetlands of equal size and like vegetation may be in the right landscape position to retain sediments. One, however, may be downstream of a land-clearing operation that has generated considerable suspended sediments in the water column, while the other is downstream from an undisturbed forest. The former should be actively performing sediment trapping in a major way, whereas the latter is not. Yet if land-clearing takes place in the latter area, the second wetland will likely trap sediments as well as the first wetland. The entire analysis typically tends to ignore opportunity since such opportunity may have occurred in the past or may occur in the future and the wetland is there to perform this service at higher levels when necessary.

W-PAWF also does not consider the condition of the adjacent upland (e.g., level of disturbance) or the actual water quality of the associated waterbody that may be regarded as important metrics for assessing the health of individual wetlands. Collection and analysis of these data may be done as a follow-up investigation, where desired.

It is important to re-emphasize that the preliminary assessment does not obviate the need for more detailed assessments of the various functions and assessment of wetland condition and opportunities to provide more benefits given the state of the contributing watershed and adjacent land use activities. This preliminary assessment should be viewed as a starting point for more rigorous assessments, since it attempts to cull out wetlands that may likely provide significant functions based on generally accepted principles and the source information used for this analysis. This assessment is most useful for regional or watershed planning purposes, for a cursory screening of sites for acquisition, and to aid in developing landscape-level wetland conservation and protection strategies. It can also be used to evaluate cumulative impacts on wetlands on key functions as was done for the Nanticoke River watershed on the Delmarva Peninsula (Tiner 2005b) or to consider the national and regional-scale impacts of policy changes on certain wetland types (e.g., geographically isolated wetlands or headwater wetlands, or determining significant nexus to waters of the United States). For site-specific evaluations, additional work will be required, especially field verification and collection of site-specific data for potential functions (e.g., following the hydrogeomorphic assessment approach as described by Brinson 1993a or other onsite evaluation procedures, e.g., rapid field assessment). This is particularly true for assessments of fish and wildlife habitats and biodiversity. Other sources of data may exist to help refine some of the findings of this report (e.g., state natural heritage data). Additional modeling could be done, for example, to identify habitats of likely significance to individual species of animals based on their specific life history requirements (see U.S. Fish and Wildlife Service 2003 for Gulf of Maine habitat analysis).

Also note that the criteria used for the relationships were based on Georgia's application of the Service's wetland classification (Cowardin et al. 1979). Regional applications of this system may differ slightly depending on regional priorities, level of field effort, and knowledge of wetland ecology. Use of the relationships in other regions of the country therefore may require some adjustment based on these considerations.

Through this analysis, numerous wetlands are predicted to perform a given function at a significant level presumably important to a watershed's ability to provide that function. "Significance" is a relative term and is used in this analysis to identify wetlands that are likely to perform a given function at a high or moderate level. It is also emphasized that the assessment is limited to wetlands (i.e., areas classified as wetlands on NWI maps). Deepwater habitats and streams were not included in the assessment, although their inherent value to wetlands and many wetland-dependent organisms is apparent.

Rationale for Preliminary Functional Assessments

The W-PAWF approach ("watershed-based preliminary assessment of wetland functions") is intended to produce a more expansive characterization of wetlands and their likely functions and data that can be used to help rank wetlands for acquisition, protection, or other purposes. Presently, a maximum of eleven functions may be evaluated: 1) surface water detention, 2) coastal storm surge detention, 3) streamflow maintenance, 4) nutrient transformation, 5) carbon sequestration, 6) sediment and other particulate retention, 7) bank and shoreline stabilization, 8) provision of fish and aquatic invertebrate habitat, 9) provision of waterfowl and waterbird habitat, 10) provision of other wildlife habitat, and 11) provision of habitat for unique, uncommon, or highly diverse wetland plant communities. The criteria used for identifying wetlands of significance for each of these functions using Georgia's NWIPlus database are discussed below. The criteria and ratings were initially developed for northeastern wetlands by the author of this report based on his knowledge of wetland characteristics and functions. The draft criteria were then reviewed and modified for various watersheds based on comments from wetland specialists working on specific watersheds in four Northeast states (Maine, New York, Delaware, and Maryland). While many of the criteria are universally applicable, when applying NWIPlus data to other regions for landscape-level functional assessment, the criteria and ratings should be reviewed. For coastal Georgia, a workshop sponsored by the Georgia Department of Natural Resources was conducted on August 31, 2010 to get input from local experts on the applicability of these relationships for tidal and nontidal wetlands in six coastal counties (see Acknowledgments for participants). The actual application of the Cowardin et al. (1979) classification also needed to be considered as there may be differences in the level of classification for individual projects, such as the use of water regime indicators that could affect functional ratings.

In developing a protocol for designating wetlands of potential significance, wetland size was generally disregarded from the criteria, with few exceptions (i.e., other wildlife habitat and biodiversity functions). This approach was followed because it was felt that individual agencies and organizations using the digital database and charged with setting priorities should make the decision on appropriate size criteria as a means of limiting the number of priority wetlands as necessary. There is no science-based size limit to establish significance for any function. However, it is obvious that, all things being equal, a larger wetland will have a higher capacity to perform a given function than a smaller one of the same type, although it is recognized that certain wildlife species (e.g., amphibians) require a multitude of small wetlands to maintain their local populations given vagaries of weather and its effect on habitat suitability.

After discussing a particular function and the wetland types that are likely to perform that function, a list of wetland types is given for two levels of function. These types were determined to have the potential to perform the subject function at a significant level.

ATTENTION: *The types that are <u>underlined</u> are types that were actually mapped during the inventory and will be displayed on the wetland function maps for coastal Georgia. The other types (not underlined) are other wetlands that may perform that function at the specified level, however no wetlands were classified as these types during this survey.*

Surface Water Detention

This function is important for reducing downstream flooding and lowering flood heights, both of which aid in minimizing property damage and personal injury from such events. In a landmark study on the relationships between wetlands and flooding at the watershed scale, Novitzki (1979) found that watersheds with 40 percent coverage by lakes and wetlands had significantly reduced flood flows -- lowered by as much as 80 percent -- compared to similar watersheds with no or few lakes and wetlands in Wisconsin. The same principles apply to Georgia where studies have shown that watersheds with an abundance of wetlands moderate flood flows more than those with less wetland (Wharton 1970). After heavy rains, the former watersheds take longer to reach peak water levels and have less fluctuation than the latter watersheds which reach their peaks more quickly, produce higher peaks, and tend to have more swift flows.

For purposes of landscape-level functional assessment following W-PAWF, this function will be restricted to surface water storage of nontidal waters. Floodplain wetlands and other lotic wetlands (basin and flat types) provide this function at significant levels. While tidal wetlands along rivers serve at times to attenuate freshwater flood flows from upstream watersheds, they are excluded from this function because they are subjected to frequent tidal flooding. The water storage function of tidal wetlands for detaining storm surges is evaluated separately via the coastal storm surge detention function. Stormwater detention ponds are designed for temporary storage of surface water and are recognized as having a high level of performance for this function.

Wetlands dominated by trees and/or dense stands of shrubs could be deemed to provide a higher level of this function than emergent wetlands, since woody vegetation (with higher frictional resistance) may further aid in flood desynchronization. However, emergent wetlands along waterways provide significant flood storage, so no distinction is made regarding the type of vegetative cover. Floodplain width could also be an important factor in evaluating the significance of performance of this function by individual wetlands (e.g., for acquisition or strengthened protection), but there is no scientifically based criterion for establishing a significance threshold based on size. Drier-end wetlands (e.g., flats), and isolated basins are rated as having moderate potential.

For this function, the following relationships are used:

High	Lentic Basin, <u>Lentic Fringe</u>, Lentic Island (basin and fringe), Lentic Flat associated with reservoirs and flood control dams, <u>Lotic Stream Basin</u>, <u>Lotic Floodplain-basin</u>, Lotic River Fringe, Lotic Stream Fringe (not "A" water regime), Lotic River Island-basin, <u>Ponds Throughflow (in-stream) and associated Fringe and Basin wetlands,</u> Terrene Throughflow Basin, <u>Stormwater Treatment Ponds</u>

Moderate	<u>Lotic River Floodplain-flat</u>, Lotic River Fringe (other than above), Lotic Stream Fringe (other than above), <u>Lotic Stream Flat</u>, Lotic River Island-flat, Lentic Flat, <u>Other Terrene Basins</u>, <u>Other Ponds and associated wetlands (excluding sewage treatment ponds and isolated impoundments)</u>, <u>Terrene wetland associated with ponds (TE pd , excluding isolated diked ponds)</u>, <u>Terrene Flat</u>

Note: Exclude the following: 1) artificially flooded wetlands ("K" water regime, unless they are in a reservoir or dammed lake), 2) isolated impounded ponds and associated wetlands, 3) any freshwater tidal wetlands that are in the Lotic landscape position, and 4) any seasonally saturated wetlands ("B" water regime) from this function.

Coastal Storm Surge Detention

This function is listed separately from Surface Water Detention to highlight the importance of tidal wetlands and adjacent lowland wetlands at storing tidal waters brought into estuaries by storms (e.g., tropical storms and hurricanes). Estuarine and freshwater tidal wetlands are important areas for temporary storage of this water. Some nontidal wetlands contiguous to these wetlands (e.g., low-lying terrene outflow basins - flatwoods) may also provide this function, but do so only during the most extreme storm events, so they were rated as moderate for this function. Note that tidal wetlands along rivers may also be important for attenuating freshwater floodwaters resulting from heavy precipitation events upstream in the watershed.

For this function, the following relationships are used:

High	<u>Estuarine Basin</u>, <u>Estuarine Fringe</u>, <u>Estuarine Island</u>, <u>Lotic Tidal Fringe</u>, Lotic Tidal Island, <u>Lotic Tidal Floodplain</u>, <u>Marine Fringe</u>, <u>Marine Island</u>
Moderate	<u>Other tidal wetlands not included above plus any Terrene wetland (excluding SL – slope wetland) with "ed" modifier (nontidal wetlands contiguous with estuarine wetlands discharging and likely subject to infrequent or occasional flooding by storm tides) or with "ow" modifier (overwash)</u>

Streamflow Maintenance

There are four main sources of water to support stream flow: 1) groundwater, 2) interflow through the soil, 3) precipitation, and 4) surface water runoff. Groundwater provides water for base flows. Many wetlands are sources of groundwater discharge and those located in headwater positions either the source of streams or along low-order perennial streams contribute significantly to sustain streamflow in the watershed. Such wetlands are critically important for supporting aquatic life in streams. The importance of maintaining natural streamflow patterns is important to riparian vegetation as well as to resident aquatic species and altering those patterns can negatively impact local biodiversity (Cowell and Stoudt 2002).

10

All wetlands classified as headwater wetlands are important for streamflow. Terrene headwater wetlands, by definition, are sources of streams. They contribute groundwater (base flow) from local unconfined aquifers and regional confined aquifers to support streamflow (Priest 2004). Other headwater wetlands include lotic wetlands along 1st-order streams and lentic wetlands associated with outflow lakes. Wetlands along 2nd-order streams in mountainous areas may be classified as headwater wetlands as they probably are sites of groundwater discharge, but these conditions do not apply to the Georgia coastal region since Georgia's mountains are much further inland. Ditched headwater wetlands are rated as moderate, since this alteration typically results in faster release of water, thereby reducing the period of outflow. Outflow from groundwater-fed wetlands (lacking a stream) may discharge directly into streams and thereby contribute variable quantities of water for sustaining baseflows. These wetlands were rated as moderate for this function. Lakes may also be important regulators of streamflow, so lentic wetlands may be designated as significant to streamflow, with those in headwater positions being rated high and others as moderate.

Floodplain wetlands are known to store water in the form of bank storage, later releasing this water to maintain baseflows (Whiting 1998). Among several key factors affecting bank storage are porosity and permeability of the bank material, the width of the floodplain, and the hydraulic gradient (steepness of the water table). It is recognized that the wider the floodplain, the more bank storage given the same soils. Gravel floodplains drain in days, sandy floodplains in a few weeks to a few years, silty floodplains in years, and clayey floodplains in decades. In good water years, wide sandy floodplains may help maintain baseflows. Bank stratigraphy is another factor that could be considered important for streamflow maintenance (Christopher Cirmo, pers. comm. 2006). For example, the presence of a "sand" layer between clay layers (such as in a system where there have been historical floods) may affect the transmissivity of the bank. Bank storage may serve to maintain streamflow in some fringe or floodplain wetlands, however a rudimentary knowledge of the surficial stratigraphy is not normally available based solely on remote data interpretation. Despite the variability in floodplain properties, the W-PAWF assessment treats all nontidal floodplain wetlands and stream basins as having potential to support streamflow, since remote sensing data does not include soil examinations or bank stratigraphy and there is no recognized floodplain width designated to separate high from moderate potential.

While diked ponds may contribute to streamflow when water overflows spillways or exceeds height of water-control structures, these ponds typically reduce streamflow (McMurray 2007, Van Liew 2004). However, some ponds may extend storm-flow over longer durations by reducing peak flows (Bosch et al. 2003). Since impounded ponds are artificially created waters that substantially alter natural streamflow characteristics they are not included as significant for streamflow maintenance.

For this function, the following relationships are used:

    High   Unaltered Headwater Wetlands and Headwater Ponds (latter are
                  natural ponds not created or altered)

Moderate   <u>Ditched or excavated Headwater Wetlands (not impounded), Lotic River (nontidal) Floodplain (excluding impounded or ditched), Lotic Stream (nontidal) Basin (excluding impounded or ditched), Terrene Basin Outflow wetlands (associated with streams not major rivers; excluding impounded or ditched)</u>

<u>Note</u>: Diked wetlands and ponds and excavated ponds should be excluded from this function.

<u>Special Note</u>: All wetlands important for streamflow maintenance should be considered to also be important for fish and aquatic invertebrates as they are vital to sustaining streamflow necessary for the survival of these aquatic organisms.

Nutrient Transformation

All wetlands recycle nutrients, but those having a fluctuating water table and corresponding changes from aerobic to anaerobic conditions are best able to recycle nitrogen and other nutrients. While vegetation slows the flow of water causing deposition of mineral and organic particles with adsorbed nutrients (nitrogen and phosphorus), hydric soils are the places where chemical transformations occur (Carter 1996). Microbial action in the soil is the driving force behind chemical transformations in wetlands. Microbes need a food source to survive and reproduce and in wetlands organic matter provides this needed sustenance. Wetlands with high amounts of organic matter should have an abundance of microflora to perform the nutrient cycling function. Wetlands are so effective at filtering and transforming nutrients that artificial wetlands are constructed for water quality renovation (e.g., Hammer 1992). Natural wetlands performing this function help improve local water quality of streams and other watercourses. Oyster reefs are also recognized as important components for nitrogen cycling in estuaries (Dame et al. 1985, Dame and Libes 1993, Fulford et al. 2010).

Numerous studies have demonstrated the importance of wetlands in denitrification. Simmons et al. (1992) found high nitrate removal (greater than 80%) from groundwater during both the growing season and dormant season in Rhode Island streamside (lotic) wetlands. Groundwater temperatures throughout the dormant season were between 6.5 and 8.0 degrees C, so microbial activity was not limited by temperature. Even the nearby upland, especially transitional areas with somewhat poorly drained soils, experienced an increase in nitrogen removal during the dormant season. This was attributed to a seasonal rise in the water table that exposed the upper portion of the groundwater to soil with more organic matter (nearer the ground surface), thereby supporting microbial activity and denitrification. Riparian forests dominated by wetlands have a greater proportion of groundwater (with nitrate) moving within the biologically active zone of the soil that makes nitrate available for uptake by plants and microbes (Nelson et al. 1995). Riparian forests on well-drained soils are much less effective at removing nitrate. In a Rhode Island study, Nelson et al. (1995) found that November had the highest nitrate removal rate due to the highest water tables in the poorly drained soils, while June experienced the lowest removal rate when the deepest water table levels occurred. Similar results can be expected to occur elsewhere. For bottomland hardwood wetlands, DeLaune et al. (1996) reported decreases in nitrate from 59-82 percent after 40 days of flooding wetland soil cores taken from the Cache River floodplain in Arkansas. Moreover, they surmised that denitrification in these soils appeared to be carbon-limited: increased denitrification took place in soils with more organic matter in the surface layer. Nitrogen removal rates for freshwater wetlands are very high (averaging from 20-80 grams/square meter) (Bowden 1987).

12

Nitrogen fixation has been attributed to blue-green algae in the photic zone at the soil-water interface and to heterotrophic bacteria associated with plant roots (Buresh et al. 1980). In working with rice, Matsuguchi (1979) believed that the significance of heterotrophic fixation in the soil layer beyond the roots has been underrated and presented data showing that such zones were the most important sites for nitrogen fixation in a Japanese rice field. This conclusion was further supported by Wada et al. (1978). Higher fixation rates have been found in the rhizosphere of wetland plants than in dryland plants. Nitrogen fixation converts atmospheric nitrogen to a usable form for plants and helps enrich soils. Plants with the ability to fix nitrogen (e.g., with symbiotic bacteria on root nodules) can thereby grow in otherwise inhospitable nutrient-poor soils.

From the water quality standpoint, wetlands associated with watercourses are probably the most noteworthy. Numerous studies have found that forested wetlands along rivers and streams ("riparian forested wetlands") are important for nutrient retention and sedimentation during floods (Whigham et al. 1988; Yarbro et al. 1984; Simpson et al. 1983; Peterjohn and Correll 1982). This function by forested riparian wetlands is especially important in agricultural areas. Brinson (1993b) suggested that riparian wetlands along low-order streams may be more important for nutrient retention than those along higher order streams.

Most of the groundwater flux from uplands to surface waters occurs in the non-growing season in the Northeast and reasonable denitrification rates occur in spring and fall making sites that are wet during these times important for nutrient retention (Art Gold, pers. comm. 2003). Wetlands with seasonally flooded and wetter water regimes (including tidal regimes - seasonally flooded-tidal, irregularly flooded, and regularly flooded) are identified as having potential to recycle nutrients at high levels of performance. The soils of these wetlands should have substantial amounts of organic matter near the surface to promote microbial activity and denitrification when wet. Based on field observations, in general, there is a positive correlation between the amount of organic matter and the degree of wetness as reflected by the NWI's water regime classification in wetlands of the Nanticoke River watershed in Delaware (Amy Jacobs, pers. comm. 2003). Periodically flooded soils also retain sediments and their adsorbed nutrients.

Drier-end wetlands -- those with a temporarily flooded water regime (including temporarily flooded-tidal) and others with a seasonally saturated water regime -- are considered as having moderate potential for performing this function, since they are relatively dry for most of the year.

For this function, relationships are the following:

High	Vegetated wetlands (and mixes with nonvegetated wetlands or unconsolidated bottom; only where vegetated predominates) with seasonally flooded (C), semipermanently flooded (F), semipermanently flooded-tidal (T), seasonally flooded-tidal (R), irregularly flooded (P), regularly flooded (N), and permanently flooded (H or L) water regimes, estuarine intertidal oyster reefs, Vegetated wetlands with a *permanently saturated* water regime
Moderate	Vegetated wetlands with *seasonally saturated* (B *on the coastal plain*), temporarily flooded (A) or temporarily flooded-tidal (S)

water regimes; nonvegetated/vegetated wetlands (where nonvegetated predominates) with seasonally flooded (C), semipermanently flooded (F), semipermanently flooded-tidal (T), seasonally flooded-tidal (R), irregularly flooded (P), regularly flooded (N), and permanently flooded (H or L) water regimes

Carbon Sequestration

Concern over rising global temperatures and climate change has directed attention to wetlands since they are recognized as important carbon sinks. Drainage of wetlands releases carbon to the atmosphere in the form of carbon dioxide, one of several greenhouse gases influencing global temperatures. In wetlands, organic matter (carbon) accumulates in the soils as well as in vegetation. Woody plants, thereby, store carbon for longer periods than annual herbaceous plants. While the above-ground biomass of perennial herbs is released back into the aquatic ecosystem seasonally, the below-ground biomass remains in the substrate and contributes to longer-term storage. Temperate and subtropical wetlands are recognized as important for attenuating global warming (Whiting and Chanton 2001).

Interestingly, tidal salt marshes sequester up to fifty times more carbon per acre than is sequestered by tropical forests (Pidgeon 2009). Salt marshes, unlike freshwater wetlands, do not release significant quantities of methane (a recognized greenhouse gas contributing to global warming) to the atmosphere (Chmura 2009). Studies in Georgia have found that among tidal wetlands, the tidal freshwater wetlands and brackish marshes sequester more carbon and retain more nutrients than salt marshes (Loomis and Craft 2010). In fact, tidal fresh and brackish marshes sequestered 66 percent of the carbon and 69 percent of the nitrogen stored in all tidal wetlands in the three-river system studied (Ogeechee, Altamaha, and Satilla) even though they represent only 41 percent of the marsh area. Anaerobic conditions resulting from prolonged flooding or soil saturation typically lead to an accumulation of organic matter. Therefore, wetlands that experience longer duration of soil saturation should accumulate more organic matter. Northern bogs that are nearly continuous saturated in boreal to arctic climates where low evapotranspiration rates occur are recognized as major global carbon sinks. Consequently, wetlands with the wetter water regimes (i.e., seasonally flooded and wetter) should store more carbon than wetlands in the same region with drier water regimes that promote more oxidation and decomposition of organic matter. Seasonally flooded and wetter vegetated wetlands are rated as high for the carbon sequestration function, while drier wetlands (temporarily flooded and seasonally saturated) are assigned a moderate rating. Tidal flats (unconsolidated shores, mudflats in particular, except sandy beaches and sand flats) are listed as moderate because they sequester carbon at lower rates than vegetated coastal wetlands (Duarte et al. 2005). Ponds were also designated as moderate because recent studies have indicated the cumulative importance of small ponds in sequestering carbon through sedimentation processes (Downing 2010). Several types of ponds that are not likely to be capture organic-enriched sediment from local watersheds are excluded from this function: aquaculture, commercial, industrial, residential-stormwater, sewage treatment, and isolated diked ponds (impoundments).

High	Tidal vegetated wetlands (including mixed with unconsolidated shore), Nontidal vegetated wetlands that are seasonally flooded, semipermanently flooded, or intermitttently exposed, Nontidal vegetated wetlands that are permanently saturated

Moderate   Nontidal vegetated wetlands that are temporarily flooded or seasonally saturated, Tidal unconsolidated shore wetlands (including mixes with vegetated types; focus on mudflats and organic substrates for purely nonvegetated types; exclude sandy beaches, sand flats, and flats with other substrates), Nontidal nonvegetated/vegetated wetlands, Ponds (excluding aquaculture, commercial, industrial, residential-stormwater, and sewage treatment ponds plus isolated impoundments)

Retention of Sediment and Other Particulates

Many wetlands owe their existence to being located in areas of sediment deposition. This is especially true for floodplain and estuarine wetlands. This function supports water quality maintenance by capturing sediments with bonded nutrients or heavy metals as in and downstream of urban areas (e.g., Gambrell 1994). Estuarine and floodplain wetlands plus lotic (streamside) and lentic (lakeshore) fringe and basin wetlands including lotic (in-stream) ponds are likely to trap and retain sediments and particulates at significant levels. Terrene throughflow basins should function similarly. Vegetated wetlands will likely favor sedimentation over nonvegetated wetlands and therefore they received a high rating versus moderate for the nonvegetated types. Lotic flat wetlands are flooded only for brief periods and less frequently than the wetlands listed above due to their elevation; they are classified as having moderate potential for sediment retention. Throughflow (in-stream) ponds and associated fringe and basin vegetated wetlands are rated as high, since they occur within the stream network where they trap water-borne sediments. Stormwater treatment ponds are designed specifically to perform this function, so they are rated as high. Other ponds and terrene basins may be locally significant in retaining such materials, and are therefore designated as moderate. However, commercial, industrial, residential, sewage treatment, golf, and mining ponds were not rated as significant since many are isolated diked impoundments. Terrene flats are not rated as potentially significant because they are level landscapes that do not appear to trap substantial amounts of sediment from surrounding areas.

For this function, the following relationships are used:

High   Estuarine vegetated (not floating mats), Lentic vegetated (not Flat and not floating mats), Lotic vegetated (not Flat, not Floodplain-flat, and not floating mats), Throughflow Ponds and Lakes (in-stream; designated as PUB... on NWI) and associated vegetated wetlands, Bidirectional-tidal Ponds and associated vegetated wetlands, Terrene Throughflow Basin, Stormwater Treatment Ponds

Moderate   Estuarine nonvegetated (excluding rocky shore), Lotic nonvegetated, Lotic Flat, Lotic Floodplain-flat, Lentic Flat, Marine Fringe (excluding rocky shore), Marine Island (excluding rocky shore), Other Terrene Basins, Terrene wetlands associated with ponds (excluding some types of ponds - commercial, industrial, sewage treatment, and mining), Other Ponds and Lakes (classified as PUB... on NWI) and associated wetlands (excluding

15

some types of ponds – commercial, industrial, sewage treatment, and mining and slope wetlands)

Bank and Shoreline Stabilization

Vegetation colonizing banks and shorelines stabilizes the soil or substrate and diminishes wave action, thereby reducing shoreline erosion potential and increasing bank stability. Vegetated wetlands along all flowing or large standing waterbodies (e.g., estuaries, lakes, rivers, and streams) therefore provide this function at high levels. Intertidal oyster reefs when located along shorelines help protect the shorelines from erosion and are therefore rated as high. Vegetated wetlands along ponds are designated as moderate for this function since there is less wave or erosive action along these shores. Since island wetlands are surrounded by water, they are not considered significant for this function. It is recognized that some wetland islands may when positioned offshore in close proximity to the shoreline reduce wave action and contribute to shoreline stabilization.

For this function, the following relationships are used:

High	Estuarine vegetated wetlands (except island types), Estuarine nonvegetated irregularly flooded, Lotic wetlands (vegetated except island and isolated types and floating mats), Lentic wetlands (vegetated except island types and floating mats)
Moderate	Other Estuarine nonvegetated wetlands (except island), Terrene vegetated wetlands associated with ponds (e.g., Fringe-pond, Flat-pond, and Basin-pond), Estuarine intertidal oyster reefs (along the shoreline), Marine Unconsolidated Shore, Terrene Outflow Headwater wetlands

Provision of Fish and Aquatic Invertebrate Habitat[1]

Wetlands are widely recognized as important habitats for many species of fish and wildlife and there is a wide body of literature to support this claim (e.g., Mitsch and Gosselink 2007, Tiner 2005a). The assessment of potential habitat for fish and aquatic invertebrates is based on generalities that could be refined for particular species of interest by others at a later date if desirable. Regional and local variations will need to be accounted for on a watershed-by-watershed basis. The criteria selected below are useful for the Georgia coastal zone and many may be applicable nationwide, but they should be re-examined for each project area beyond the Georgia coast to ensure accuracy and completeness. Although focused on fish and aquatic invertebrates, wetlands identified as significant for these species are likely also significant for other aquatic-dependent animals such as muskrat, turtles, water snakes, and numerous amphibians.

For tidal areas, the assessment emphasizes estuarine wetlands, palustrine and riverine tidal emergent wetlands, unconsolidated shores (tidal flats), and intertidal oyster reefs. For nontidal regions, palustrine aquatic beds and permanently flooded and semipermanently flooded wetlands

---

[1] This assessment is focused on wetlands, not deepwater habitats, hence the exclusion of the latter from this analysis, despite widespread recognition that rivers, streams, and lakes are the primary habitats for fish and shellfish.

16

are ranked higher than seasonally flooded types due to the longer duration of surface water. Semipermanently flooded wetlands along permanent waterbodies may serve as fish spawning grounds during high flows. Many ponds (excluding wastewater ponds, for example) and the shallow marsh-open water zone of impoundments are identified as wetlands having moderate potential for fish and aquatic invertebrate habitat.

Shading by trees and tall shrubs moderates water temperatures for streams (Ghermandi et al. 2009, Wilkerson et al. 2006). Since water temperature is an important factor influencing fish use of streams as well as providing food (through leaf drop) for aquatic organisms that are an important part of the diet of juvenile and some adult fishes, forested and shrub wetlands along streams have been rated as moderate for fish and shellfish. The streamside wetlands also serve as vital buffers that help maintain good water quality.

Other wetlands providing significant fish habitat or benefits to their habitat may exist, but are not identified. Such wetlands may be identified based on actual observations or culled out from site-specific fisheries information that may be available from other sources. Moreover, all wetlands rated as significant for the streamflow maintenance function are already considered vital to sustaining the watershed's ability to provide lotic aquatic habitat. While these wetlands may not serve as significant fish and shellfish habitat, they support base flows essential to keeping water in streams for aquatic life. Terrene outflow wetlands and Lotic basin wetlands along low order streams (e.g., orders 1-2 in Coastal Plain) often discharge cool groundwater to streams which keeps these streams cooler in summer. Such wetlands are important for providing summer refuges for some species.

For this function, the following relationships are used:

High	Estuarine Emergent Wetland (including mixtures with other types where emergent is the dominant class), Estuarine Unconsolidated Shore (not irregularly flooded type), Estuarine Intertidal Reef (oyster), Estuarine Aquatic Bed, Lacustrine Littoral semipermanently flooded or permanently flooded (excluding wetlands along intermittent streams), Lacustrine Littoral Aquatic Bed, Lacustrine Littoral Unconsolidated Bottom/Vegetated Wetland, Marine Intertidal Unconsolidated Shore (not irregularly flooded), Palustrine semipermanently flooded (excluding wetlands along intermittent streams; *must be contiguous with a permanent waterbody* such as PUBH, L1UBH, or R2/R3UBH *or be a semipermanently flooded slough*), Palustrine Aquatic Bed, Palustrine Unconsolidated Bottom/Vegetated Wetland, Palustrine Vegetated Wetland with a permanently flooded water regime, Palustrine Tidal Emergent Wetland (excluding S water regime), Ponds (PUBH… on NWI; not PUBF) associated with semipermanently flooded or permanently flooded Vegetated Wetland, Riverine Tidal Emergent Wetland, Riverine Tidal Unconsolidated Shore (excluding those with an S water regime), Riverine Tidal Aquatic Bed, Riverine Lower Perennial Aquatic Bed, Riverine Lower Perennial Aquatic Bed

Moderate	Estuarine Wetlands where Forested or Scrub-Shrub Wetland is mixed with Emergent Wetland, Lentic wetlands that are PEM1C (and contiguous with a waterbody), Lotic River or Stream wetlands that are PEM1C (including mixtures with Scrub-Shrub or Forested wetlands; and contiguous with a waterbody), Other Ponds and associated Fringe wetlands (i.e., one acre or larger; specify pond types: natural ponds, beaver ponds, and excavated or impounded ponds that are used for aquaculture and wildlife management), Lotic River Floodplain Basin Wetlands, Palustrine Tidal Forested or Scrub-Shrub Wetlands mixed with Emergent Wetland with seasonally flooded-tidal (R) or semipermanently flooded-tidal (T) water regimes

Note: Industrial, commercial, and wastewater treatment ponds should be excluded from this function.

Provision of Waterfowl and Waterbird Habitat

Wetlands designated as important for waterfowl (e.g., ducks, geese, and loons) and waterbirds (e.g., wading birds, shorebirds, rails, marsh wrens, and red-winged blackbirds) are generally those used for nesting, reproduction, or feeding. The emphasis is on the wetter wetlands and ones that are frequently flooded for long periods. Other birds dependent on and/or living in other wetlands (e.g., waterthrushes, veery, eastern kingbird, vireos, and warblers) are not included in this function; they are included in the large group of animals referred to as "other wildlife" in this assessment.

The selected wetlands include estuarine wetlands (vegetated or not), riverine emergent wetlands, estuarine and riverine unconsolidated shores (excluding temporary flooded-tidal), palustrine tidal and riverine tidal emergent wetlands (including emergent/shrub mixtures), semipermanently flooded wetlands, mixed open water-emergent wetlands (palustrine and lacustrine), and aquatic beds. Seasonally flooded lotic wetlands that are forested or mixtures of trees and shrubs (excluding those along intermittent streams) are designated as having high potential because they offer prime habitats for wood ducks. For this analysis, palustrine tidal scrub-shrub/emergent wetlands and tidal forested/emergent wetlands were designated as having moderate significance for waterfowl and waterbirds. Similar mixed wetlands dominated by emergent species, however, are listed as having high significance, since the emergents typically represent wetter conditions in Georgia's tidal zone. Ponds one acre and larger were considered to have moderate potential for providing waterfowl and waterbird habitat.[2] Semipermanently flooded vegetated wetlands that were not associated with a waterbody were rated as moderate for this function as were seasonally flooded emergent wetlands (including mixtures with shrubs) contiguous with water bodies.

---

[2]Ponds on wildlife management areas (e.g., refuges) should be considered to be of high significance due to their management. Since we do not presently have the location of refuges recorded in our digital database, these ponds may not be separated from the rest of the ponds. Hence, all ponds except industrial, commercial, stormwater detention, wastewater treatment, and similar ponds, are designated as having moderate potential for this function.

For this function, the following relationships are used:

High   Estuarine Aquatic Bed, <u>Estuarine Emergent wetlands (including mixtures with other vegetated types where EM dominates, e.g., EM/SS), Estuarine Unconsolidated Shore (except S water regime),</u> Estuarine Intertidal Reef, <u>Lacustrine Semipermanently Flooded, Lacustrine Littoral Aquatic Bed (and mixes where AB dominates),</u> Lacustrine Littoral Vegetated wetlands with an H water regime, <u>Lacustrine Unconsolidated Shores (F, E, or C water regimes), Marine Unconsolidated Shore, Palustrine Semipermanently Flooded and adjacent to a waterbody or along a slough; Palustrine Semipermanently Flooded-Tidal, Palustrine Aquatic Bed,</u> Palustrine Vegetated wetlands with an H water regime, Seasonally Flooded Palustrine wetlands impounded (all vegetation types and associated PUB waters – natural ponds, waterfowl/wildlife impoundments, and beaver ponds), Lotic River or Stream wetlands that are PEM1C (including mixtures with Scrub-Shrub or Forested wetlands), <u>Ponds associated with Semipermanently Flooded Vegetated wetlands, Palustrine Tidal Emergent wetlands (PEM1R and PEM1T and mixes with other EM and with SS and FO),</u> Riverine Tidal Emergent wetlands, <u>Riverine Tidal Unconsolidated Shores (except with S water regime), Ponds associated with all of the above wetland types,</u> Lotic Basin or Fringe or Floodplain-basin wetlands (excluding those along intermittent streams) that are Forested or Scrub-shrub or mixtures of these types with C, F, R, or H water regime; Lotic wetlands that are mixed Forested/Emergent or Unconsolidated Bottom/Forested with a F, R, or H water regime; <u>Palustrine Tidal Forested or Scrub-shrub wetlands (and mixes with other types like the Lotic types) in Estuarine reach with R or N water regime</u> and contiguous with open Water, <u>Wildlife Impoundments ("wi")</u>

Moderate Estuarine Scrub-Shrub/Emergent wetland Oligohaline, Seasonally Flooded-Tidal Palustrine Wetland where EM is the subordinate mixed class (e.g., PFO1/EM1R), <u>Ponds 1 acre or greater in size (excluding industrial, commercial, stormwater detention, wastewater treatment, and similar ponds),</u> Palustrine Emergent wetlands (including mixtures with Scrub-shrub) that are Seasonally Flooded and associated with permanently flooded waterbodies, <u>Other Palustrine vegetated (AB, EM, SS, FO) wetlands that are Semipermanently Flooded, Other Lacustrine Littoral Unconsolidated Bottom wetlands</u>

<u>Note</u>: All waterfowl impoundments and associated wetlands that should be marked with "wi" should be rated as high for this function. Ponds used for aquaculture are excluded since management will likely deter use of these ponds; associated wetlands should also be excluded from this function. Industrial, commercial, and wastewater treatment ponds, lakes, and associated wetlands should be excluded from this function.

Provision of Other Wildlife Habitat

The provision of other wildlife habitat by wetlands was evaluated in general terms. Species-specific habitat requirements were not considered. In developing an evaluation method for wildlife habitat in the glaciated Northeast, Golet (1972) designated several types as outstanding wildlife wetlands including: 1) wetlands with rare, restricted, endemic, or relict flora and/or fauna, 2) wetlands with unusually high visual quality and infrequent occurrence, 3) wetlands with flora and fauna at the limits of their range, 4) wetlands with several seral stages of hydrarch succession, and 5) wetlands used by great numbers of migratory waterfowl, shorebirds, marsh birds, and wading birds. Golet subscribed to the principle that in general, as wetland size increases so does wildlife value, so wetland size was important factor for determining wildlife habitat potential in his approach. Other important variables included dominant wetland class, site type (bottomland vs. upland; associated with waterbody vs. isolated), surrounding habitat type (e.g., natural vegetation vs. developed land), degree of interspersion (water vs. vegetation), wetland juxtaposition (proximity to other wetlands), and water chemistry.

For this analysis, wetlands important to waterfowl and waterbirds are identified in a separate assessment. Emphasis for assessing "other wildlife" was placed on conditions that would likely provide significant habitat for other vertebrate wildlife (mainly interior forest birds, amphibians, reptiles, and non-aquatic mammals).

Opportunistic species that are highly adaptable to fragmented landscapes are not among the target organisms, since there seems to be more than ample habitat for these species now and in the future. Rather, animals whose populations may decline as wetland habitats become fragmented by development are of key concern. For example, breeding success of neotropical migrant birds in fragmented forests of Illinois was extremely low due to high predation rates and brood parasitism by brown-headed cowbirds (Robinson 1990). Newmark (1991) reported local extinctions of forest interior birds in Tanzania due to fragmentation of tropical forests. Fragmentation of wetlands is an important issue for wildlife managers to address. Some useful references on fragmentation relative to forest birds are Askins et al. (1987), Robbins et al. (1989), Freemark and Merriam (1986), and Freemark and Collins (1992). The latter study includes a list of area-sensitive or forest interior birds for the eastern United States. The work of Robbins et al. (1989) addressed area requirements of forest birds in the Mid-Atlantic states and may be useful further south along the coastal plain. They found that species such as the black-throated blue warbler, cerulean warbler, Canada warbler, and black-and-white warbler required very large tracts of forest for breeding. Ground-nesters, such as veery, black-and-white warbler, worm-eating warbler, ovenbird, waterthrushes, and Kentucky warbler, are particularly sensitive to predation which may be increased in fragmented landscapes. Robbins et al. (1989) suggest a minimum forest size of 7,410 acres to retain all species of the forest-breeding avifauna in the Mid-Atlantic region. Schroeder (1996) noted that to conserve regional biodiversity, maintenance of large-area habitats for forest interior birds is essential. As mentioned previously, Robbins et al. (1989) suggest a minimum forest size of 7,410 acres to retain all species of the forest-breeding avifauna in the Mid-Atlantic region. Consequently, forested areas 7,000 acres and larger that contained contiguous palustrine forested wetlands and upland forests are important for maintaining regional biodiversity of avifauna on the Atlantic Coastal Plain based on recommendations by Robbins et al. (1989). Forested wetlands within large forest blocks 7,000 acres or more were rated as having potential for providing high value habitat for other wildlife.

While many amphibians are strictly aquatic animals living in water, salamanders, spring peepers, and chorus frogs spend most of their adult lives in other wetlands and upland habitats, but use open-water wetlands (including vernal pools) for breeding. For these species, small isolated permanently flooded or semipermanently flooded wetlands (including ponds) in an upland forest matrix (e.g., woodland vernal pools) have been rated as having high habitat value and other wetlands contiguous to or within 100m of these wetlands have also been similarly rated. Although this assessment focuses on wetlands, it is important to recognize that upland forests adjacent to these breeding ponds are prime habitats for the juveniles and adults of these species.

Many terrestrial mammals make use of wetlands including rabbits, raccoons, and deer. For these animals, large wetlands ($\geq$ 20 acres) regardless of vegetative cover but excluding pine plantations and smaller diverse wetlands (10-20 acres with multiple cover types) have been rated as high value. Freshwater wetlands on or near back-barrier islands (including major hammocks) are particularly valuable habitat for numerous island wildlife. Any remaining vegetated wetlands are designated as having moderate value for providing wildlife habitat.

Please note that with the exception of vernal pools (woodland ponds), ponds are not listed as important as significant for "other wildlife." Wildlife species living in ponds, such as several species of frogs and turtles, are mentioned in the discussion of fish and aquatic invertebrate habitat, since wetlands designated as important for fish and invertebrates provide required habitat for these species.

High	*Forested wetlands within 7000-acre blocks of forest, vegetated wetlands >20 acres (excluding open water, nonvegetated areas, and pine plantations), small diverse wetlands (10-20 acres with 2 or more covertypes; excluding open water as one of the covertypes), *small isolated permanently flooded or semipermanently flooded wetlands within an upland forest matrix (including small ponds that may be vernal pools) and contiguous wetlands, small vegetated wetlands on or near coastal back-barrier islands (including those on major hammocks)
Moderate	Other vegetated wetlands

*Not identified for the coastal county project.

Given the general nature of this assessment of "other wildlife habitat," other individuals may want to refine this assessment in the future by having biologists designate "target species" that may be used to identify important wildlife habitats in a particular watershed. After doing this, they could identify criteria that may be used to identify potentially significant habitat for these species in the watershed.

Provision of Unique, Uncommon, or Highly Diverse Wetland Plant Communities

This function is used to identify wetlands that are unique or uncommon wetland types in a watershed or other study area, or that represent highly diverse plant communities. All riverine and palustrine tidal emergent and scrub-shrub wetlands (regularly flooded, seasonally flooded-tidal, and semipermanently flooded-tidal) and estuarine oligohaline vegetated wetlands are identified as significant for this function because they often possess some of the most diverse wetland plant communities along the Atlantic Coast. While Phragmites-dominated wetlands are generally excluded from this listing, any wetland supporting stands of the native species should be recognized as a significant habitat. While this type was not mapped during the updated inventory, it may be added from documented occurrences if desirable. Generally, however, the use of Natural Heritage Program data and other data are beyond the scope of this remotely sensed approach to wetland functional analysis. Consequently, wetlands designated as potentially significant for this function by the W-PAWF assessment are simply a starting point or, in other words, a foundation to build upon. Local knowledge of significant wetlands and Natural Heritage Program data can be applied by others to further refine the list of wetlands important for this function for specific geographic areas.

The following are examples of wetland types viewed as potentially significant for the provision of habitat for unique or diverse wetland plant communities in coastal Georgia (Note: The ones underlined were identified during the inventory):

Significant   Estuarine oligohaline vegetated wetlands
Riverine tidal emergent wetlands (including tidal flats that are often colonized by nonpersistent plants during the growing season)
Palustrine tidal emergent wetlands (regularly flooded, seasonally flooded tidal, and semipermanently flooded-tidal water regimes)
Palustrine tidal scrub-shrub wetlands (regularly flooded, seasonally flooded-tidal, and semipermanently flooded-tidal water regimes)
Freshwater vegetated wetlands on barrier islands (semipermanently flooded, semipermanently flooded-tidal, and permanently flooded)
Brackish marshes at upper edge of salt marshes
Stands of native Phragmites (Note: These stands have not been identified in the wetland mapping, but can be identified from our sources.)
Carolina bay wetlands (relatively intact)
Palustrine vegetated wetlands permanently flooded

Summary

The State of Georgia has added descriptors for landscape position, landform, and water flow path to its updated wetland digital database for six coastal counties. When LLWW descriptors are combined with typical NWI attributes from Cowardin et al. 1979 (system, subsystem, class, subclass, water regime, and special modifiers), a NWIPlus database is created. It contains many properties for each wetland that can be used to produce a preliminary landscape-level assessment of wetland functions for large geographic areas. The subject report provides the rationale for the criteria used to identify wetlands of potential significance for eleven functions. These functions include: 1) surface water detention, 2) coastal storm surge detention, 3) streamflow maintenance, 4) nutrient transformation, 5) carbon sequestration, 6) sediment and other particulate retention, 7) bank and shoreline stabilization, 8) provision of fish and aquatic invertebrate habitat, 9) provision of waterfowl and waterbird habitat, 10) provision of other wildlife habitat, and 11) provision of habitat for unique, uncommon, or highly diverse wetland plant communities. The preliminary nature of this type of functional assessment must be emphasized and while it provides a valuable landscape-level perspective on wetland functions, field investigations are required to refine these findings for specific wetlands or areas of interest.

Acknowledgments

The Georgia relationships between NWIPlus features and eleven functions were developed with help from participants of the August 31, 2010 workshop at Little St. Simons Island. Jan Mackinnon (GA DNR, Coastal Resources Division) was instrumental in organizing the workshop. Workshop participants included: Chandra Franklin (Savannah State University), Clark Alexander (Skidaway Institute of Oceanography), Dorset Hurley (Sapelo Island National Estuarine Research Reserve), Dominic Guadagnoli (GA DNR), Gabe Gaddis (GA DNR), Deb Barreiro (GA DNR), Karl Burgess (GA DNR), Jill Andrews (Georgia Coastal Management Program), Bill Wikoff (U.S. Fish and Wildlife Service), Chris Capolla (U.S. Fish and Wildlife Service), Ralph Tiner (U.S. Fish and Wildlife Service), Brandon Moody (GA DNR Environmental Protection Agency), Brad Winn (GA DNR Wildife Resources Division), Shelly Krueger (University of Georgia, Marine Extension Service), Amanda Wrona (The Nature Conservancy), Kelly O'Rourke (Georgia Coastal Management Program), Sonny Emmert (Georgia Coastal Management Program), Dale Caldwell (GA Environmental Protection Division), Jeb Byers (University of Georgia, Odum School of Ecology), Risa Cohen (Georgia Southern University), Katy Freas (U.S. Army Corps of Engineers), Rhonda Evans (U.S. Environmental Protection Agency, Region IV), Tony Able (U.S. Environmental Protection Agency, Region IV), John Hefner (Atkins North America, formerly PBS&J, Raleigh, NC), Dave O'Loughlin (Atkins North America), Rainor Gresham (Atkins North America), Ben Cogdell (Atkins North America), Keith Parsons (GA Environmental Protection Division), Steve Calver (U.S. Army Corps of Engineers Planning Division), Susan Reeves (GA DNR), Jan Mackinnon, and Scott Coleman (Little St. Simons Island).

The draft document was reviewed by personnel from Atkins North America and the GA DNR's Coastal Resources Division. Rainor Gresham provided a listing of the wetland types that were mapped in the study area for each wetland function. This information was used to highlight those wetlands in the listing of potential wetlands of significance for each function.

The foundation for the wetland characteristics-function relationships was laid over the past 15 years and many people had a hand in the process and were recognized in the 2003 correlation report for the Northeast (Tiner 2003b). Since then additional peer review comments were subsequently provided by Dr. Robert Brooks (Pennsylvania State University), Dr. Christopher Cirmo (Cortland State University), Dr. Andrew Baldwin (University of Maryland), Dr. Mark Brinson (East Carolina University), Dr. Donald Leopold (State University of New York-Syracuse), Matt Schweisberg (U.S. EPA, Region 1), Dr. Charles Roman (U.S. Geological Survey, University of Rhode Island), and Dr. Aram Calhoun (University of Maine). Their comments were helpful in improving the document.

References

Askins, R.A., M.J. Philbrick, and D.S. Sugeno. 1987. Relationship between the regional abundance of forest and the composition of forest bird communities. Biol. Cons. 39: 129-152.

Bosch, D.D., R.R. Lowranace, J.M. Sheridan, and R.G. Williams. 2003. Ground water storage effect on streamflow for a southeastern Coastal Plain watershed. Ground Water 47(7): 903-912. http://www.tifton.uga.edu/sewrl/bosch/2003%20Bosch%20GWater%20Ground%20Water%20St orage%20Effect.pdf

Bowden, W.B. 1987. The biogeochemistry of nitrogen in freshwater wetlands. Biogeochemistry 4: 313-348.

Brinson, M. M. 1993a. A Hydrogeomorphic Classification for Wetlands. U.S. Army Corps of Engineers, Washington, DC. Wetlands Research Program, Technical Report WRP-DE-4.

Brinson, M.M. 1993b. Changes in the functioning of wetlands along environmental gradients. Wetlands 13; 65-74.

Brooks, R. P., D. H. Wardrop, and J. A. Bishop. 2004. Assessing wetland condition on a watershed basis in the Mid-Atlantic region using synoptic land cover maps. Environmental Monitoring and Assessment 94:9-22.

Buresh, R.J., M.E. Casselman, and W.H. Patrick. 1980. Nitrogen fixation in flooded soil systems, a review. Advances in Agronomy 33: 149-192.

Carter, V. 1996. Wetland hydrology, water quality, and associated functions. In: J.D. Fretwell, J.S. Williams, and P.J. Redman (compilers). National Water Summary on Wetland Resources. U.S. Geological Survey, Reston, VA. Water-Supply Paper 2425. pp. 35-48.

Chmura, G.L. 2009. Tidal salt marshes. In: D.d'A. Laffoley and G. Grimsditch (eds). The Management of Natural Coastal Carbon Sinks. International Union for Conservation of Nature, Gland, Switzerland. pp. 5-11.

Cowardin, L. M., V. Carter, F. C. Golet, and E. T. LaRoe. 1979. Classification of Wetlands and Deepwater Habitats of the United States. U.S. Fish and Wildlife Service, Washington, DC. FWS/OBS-79/31. http://library.fws.gov/FWS-OBS/79_31.pdf

Cowell, C.M. and R.T. Stoudt. 2002. Dam-induced modifications to upper Allegheny River streamflow patterns and their biodiversity implications. Journal of the American Water Resources Association 38(1): 187-196.

Dame, R., and Libes, S. 1993. Oyster Reefs and Nutrient retention in tidal creeks. Journal of Expermental Marine Biology and Ecology. 171 (2): 251-258.

Dame, R.F., T.G. Wolaver, and S.M. Libes. 1985. The summer uptake and release of nitrogen by an intertidal oyster reef. Netherlands Journal of Sea Research 19: 265-268.

DeLaune, R.D., R.R. Boar, C.W. Lindau, and B.A. Kleiss. 1996. Denitrification in bottomland hardwood wetland soils of the Cache River. Wetlands 16: 309-320.

Downing, J.A. 2010. Emerging global role of small lakes and ponds: little thing mean a lot. Limnetica 29(1): 9-24.

Duarte, C.M., J.J. Middelburg, and N. Caraco. 2005. Major role of marine vegetation on the oceanic carbon cycle. Biogeosciences 2: 1-8.

Federal Geographic Data Committee (FGDC) Wetlands Subcommittee. 2009. Wetlands mapping standard. FGDC Document Number FGDC-STD-015-2009. http://www.fgdc.gov/standards/projects/FGDC-standards-projects/wetlands-mapping/2009-08%20FGDC%20Wetlands%20Mapping%20Standard_final.pdf

Freemark, K. and B. Collins. 1992. Landscape ecology of breeding birds in temperate forest fragments. In: J.W. Hagan III and D.W. Johnston (editors). Ecology and Conservation of Neotropical Birds. Smithsonian Institution Press. pp. 443-453.

Freemark, K.E. and H.G. Merriam. 1986. Importance of area and habitat heterogenity to bird assemblages in temperate forest fragments. Biol. Cons. 36: 115-141.

Fulford, R.S., D.L. Breitburg, M.W. Luckenbach, and R.I.E. Newell. 2010. Evaluating responses of estuarine food webs to oyster restoration and nutrient load reduction with a multi-species bioenergetics model. Ecological Applications 20: 915-934.

Gambrell, R.P. 1994. Trace and toxic metals in wetlands – a review. Journal of Environmental Quality 23: 883-891.

Ghermandi, A., V. Vandenberghe, L. Benedetti, W. Bauwens, and P.A. Vanrolleghem. 2009. Model-based assessment of shading effect by riparian vegetation on river water quality. Ecological Engineering 35 (1): 92-104

Golet, F.C. 1972. Classification and Evaluation of Freshwater Wetlands as Wildlife Habitat in the Glaciated Northeast. University of Massachusetts, Amherst, MA. Ph. D. dissertation.

Hammer, D.A. 1992. Creating Freshwater Wetlands. Lewis Publishers, Inc., Chelsea, MI.

Loomis, M.J. and C. B. Craft. 2010. Carbon sequestration and nutrient (N, P) accumulation in river-dominated tidal marshes, Georgia, USA. Soil Science Society of America Journal 74: 1028-1037.

Matsuguchi, T. 1979. In: Nitrogen and Rice. International Rice Research Institute, Los Banos, Philippines. Pp. 207-222.

McMurray, D. 2007. A risk assessment of the impact of farm dams on streamflow in catchments on Kangaroo Island. Government of South Australia, Department of Water, Land and Biodiversity Conservation, Adelaide, SA. Technical Note 2007/16. http://www.environment.sa.gov.au/dwlbc/assets/files/ki_dwlbc_tech_note_2007_16.pdf

Mitsch, W.J. and J.G. Gosselink. 2007. Wetlands, 4th edition. John Wiley & Sons, Inc., New York, NY.

Nelson, W.M., A.J. Gold, and P.M. Groffman. 1995. Spatial and temporal variation in groundwater nitrate removal in a riparian forest. J. Environ. Qual. 24; 691-699.

Newmark, W.D. 1991. Tropical forest fragmentation and the local extinction of understory birds in the eastern Usambara Mountains, Tanzania. Conservation Biology 5: 67-78.

Novitzki, R.P. 1979. The hydrologic characteristics of Wisconsin wetlands and their influence on floods, streamflow, and sediment. In: P.E. Greeson et al. (editors). Wetland Functions and Values: The State of Our Understanding. Amer. Water Resources Assoc., Minneapolis, MN. pp. 377-388.

Peterjohn, W.T. and D.L. Correll. 1982. Nutrient dynamics in an agricultural watershed: observations on the role of a riparian forest. Ecology 65: 1466-1475.

Pidgeon, E. 2009. Carbon sequestration by coastal marine habitats: important missing sinks. In: D.d'A. Laffoley and G. Grimsditch (eds). The Management of Natural Coastal Carbon Sinks. International Union for Conservation of Nature, Gland, Switzerland. pp. 47-51.

Priest, S. 2004. Evaluation of ground-water contribution to streamflow in coastal Georgia and adjacent parts of Florida and South Carolina. U.S. Geological Survey, Reston, VA. Scientific Investigations Report 2004-5265.

Robbins, C.S., D.K. Dawson, and B.A. Dowell. 1989. Habitat area requirements of breeding forest birds of the Mid-Atlantic states. Wildlife Monogr. 103: 1-34.

Robinson, S.K. 1990. Effects of Forest Fragmentation on Nesting Songbirds. Illinois Natural History Survey, Champaign, IL.

Schroeder, R.L. 1996. Wildlife Community Habitat Evaluation Using a Modified Species-Area Relationship. U.S. Army Corps of Engineers, Waterways Expt. Station, Vicksburg, MS. Wetlands Research Program Tech. Rep. WRP-DE-12.

Simmons, R.C., A.J. Gold, and P.M. Groffman. 1992. Nitrate dynamics in riparian forests: groundwater studies. J. Environ. Qual. 21: 659-665.

Simpson, R.L., R.E. Good, R. Walker, and B.R. Frasco. 1983. The role of Delaware River freshwater tidal wetlands in the retention of nutrients and heavy metals. J. Environ. Qual. 12: 41-48.

Tiner, R.W. 1995. A landscape and landform classification for Northeast wetlands (an operational draft). U.S. Fish and Wildlife Service, Ecological Services, Northeast Region, Hadley, MA.

Tiner, R.W. 1996a. A landscape and landform classification for Northeast wetlands. U..S. Fish and Wildlife Service, National Wetlands Inventory Project, Northeast Region, Hadley, MA.

Tiner, R.W. 1996b. Keys to landscape position and landform descriptors for Northeast wetlands. U.S. Fish and Wildlife Service, Ecological Services, Northeast Region, Hadley, MA.

Tiner, R.W. 1997a. Keys to landscape position and landform descriptors for U.S. wetlands (operational draft). U.S. Fish and Wildlife Service, National Wetlands Inventory Program, Northeast Region, Hadley, MA.

Tiner, R.W. 1997b. Piloting a more descriptive NWI. National Wetlands Newsletter 19(5): 14-16.

Tiner, R.W. 1997c. NWI Maps: What They Tell Us. National Wetlands Newsletter 19(2): 7-12. (Copy available from USFWS, ES-NWI, 300 Westgate Center Drive, Hadley, MA 01035)

Tiner, R.W. 1999. Wetland Indicators: A Guide to Wetland Identification, Delineation, Classification, and Mapping. Lewis Publishers, CRC Press, Boca Raton, FL.

Tiner, R. W. 2000. Keys to Waterbody Type and Hydrogeomorphic-type Wetland Descriptors for U.S. Waters and Wetlands (Operational Draft). U.S. Fish and Wildlife Service, Northeast Region, Hadley, MA.

Tiner, R. W. 2002. Keys to Waterbody Type and Hydrogeomorphic-type Wetland Descriptors for U.S. Waters and Wetlands (Operational Draft). U.S. Fish and Wildlife Service, Northeast Region, Hadley, MA.

Tiner, R.W. 2003a. Dichotomous Keys and Mapping Codes for Wetland Landscape Position, Landform, Water Flow Path, and Waterbody Type Descriptors. U.S. Fish and Wildlife Service, National Wetlands Inventory Program, Northeast Region, Hadley, MA. http://library.fws.gov/Wetlands/dichotomouskeys0903.pdf

Tiner, R.W. 2003b. Correlating Enhanced National Wetlands Inventory Data with Wetland Functions for Watershed Assessments: A Rationale for Northeastern U.S. Wetlands. U.S. Fish and Wildlife Service, National Wetlands Inventory Program, Region 5, Hadley, MA. http://www.fws.gov/northeast/wetlands/pdf/CorrelatingEnhancedNWIDataWetlandFunctionsWa tershedAssessments[1].pdf

Tiner, R.W. 2005a. In Search of Swampland: A Wetland Sourcebook and Field Guide. Revised 2nd Edition. Rutgers University Press, New Brunswick, NJ.

Tiner, R.W. 2005b. Assessing cumulative loss of wetland functions in the Nanticoke River watershed using enhanced National Wetlands Inventory data. Wetlands 25(2): 405-419.

Tiner, R.W. 2010. NWIPlus: Geospatial database for watershed-level functional assessment. National Wetlands Newsletter 32(3): 4-7, 23. http://www.fws.gov/northeast/wetlands/Publications%20PDFs%20as%20of%20March_2008/Ma pping/NWIPlus_NWN.pdf

U.S. Fish and Wildlife Service. 2003. Gulf of Maine Watershed Habitat Analysis. Version 3.1. Gulf of Maine Coastal Program Office, Falmouth, MA. (http://gulfofmaine.fws.gov)

Van Liew, M.W. 2004. Impact of flood retarding structures on simulated streamflow for various sized watersheds under varying climatic conditions. GIS and Remote Sensing in Hydrology, Water Resources and Environment, Proceedings of ICGRHWE, Three Gorges Dam, China (September 2003). IAHS Publication 289: 33-40. http://iahs.info/redbooks/a289/iahs_289_0033.pdf

Wada, H., S. Panichsakpatana, M. Kimura, and Y. Takai. 1978. Soil Sci. Plant Nutr. 24: 357-365.

Wharton, C.H. 1970. The Southern River Swamp – A Multiple-use Environment. Georgia State University, School of Business Administration. Bureau of Business and Economic Research, Atlanta, GA.

Whigham, D.F., C. Chitterling, and B. Palmer. 1988. Impacts of freshwater wetlands on water quality: a landscape perspective. Environmental Management 12: 663-671.

Whiting, G.J. and J.P. Chanton. 2001. Greenhouse carbon balance of wetlands: methane emission versus carbon sequestration. Tellus B 53: 521-528.

Whiting, P.J. 1998. Bank storage and its influence on streamflow. Stream Notes July 1998. Stream Systems Technology Center, Rocky Mountain Research Station, Fort Collins, CO.

Wilkerson, E., J.M. Hagan, D. Siegel, and A.A. Whitman. 2006. The effectiveness of different buffer widths for protecting headwater stream temperature in Maine. Forest Science 52 (3): 221-231.

Yarbro, L.A., E.J. Kuenzler, P.J. Mulholland, and R.P. Sniffen. 1984. Effects of stream channelization on exports of nitrogen and phosphorus from North Carolina Coastal Plain watersheds. Environmental Management 8: 151-160.